Volume 69 of the Yale Series of Younger Poets

THREATS INSTEAD OF TREES

MICHAEL RYAN

FOREWORD BY STANLEY KUNITZ

NEW HAVEN AND LONDON

YALE UNIVERSITY PRESS, 1974

Published with assistance from
the Mary Cady Tew Memorial Fund.

Library of Congress catalog card number: 73–87737
ISBN: 0–300–01738–3 (cloth), 0–300–01739–1 (paper)

Designed by Sally Sullivan
and set in Baskerville type.
Printed in the United States of America by
The Colonial Press Inc.,
Clinton, Massachusetts.

Published in Great Britain, Europe, and Africa by
Yale University Press, Ltd., London.
Distributed in Latin America by Kaiman & Polon,
Inc., New York City; in Australasia and Southeast
Asia by John Wiley & Sons Australasia Pty. Ltd.,
Sydney; in India by UBS Publishers' Distributors Pvt.,
Ltd., Delhi; in Japan by John Weatherhill, Inc., Tokyo.

for my father

We *are* solitary. We may delude our-
selves and act as though this were not
so. But how much better it is to realize
it, yes, even to begin by assuming it.

R. M. Rilke

Even in religious fervor there is a
touch of animal heat.

Walt Whitman

Contents

III

IV

V

Acknowledgments

Acknowledgment is made to the following magazines and anthologies in which some of these poems first appeared: *Arion's Dolphin, Ark River Review, Intro/4, The Nation, The New Yorker, Northwest Review, The Ohio Review, Ploughshares, Poetry, Poetry Northwest,* and *Poetry Now.*

"A Posthumous Poetics" first appeared in *Poetry.*
"Letter from an Institution: I" first appeared in
  The New Yorker.
"Speaking" was printed as a broadside by Borogove Press.

Special thanks to my mother, Elvera Ryan, to two teachers, Ernest Sandeen and Marvin Bell, and to Patricia Hackett.

Foreword

Michael Ryan is a poet of secrets and dislocations. Every word of his counts. The air of his poems is charged and ominous. Even the love poems admit feelings of doubt and dread. Their order embraces a violent reality. He has a mind that rejoices in the play of concepts, in the embodiment of "thought as experience." The imagination that presides over his work is elusive, complex, and singularly restless.

At the traumatic center of a young man's world is the death of the father. In poem after poem Ryan returns to this theme, no matter from what starting point, partly because it is what his memory most fears, partly because it is that event by which he is renewed. In "The Beginning of Sympathy" he writes:

I've never left my father.
He's getting colder,
his voice thin as an angel's,
although his tongue is stuck in death.
Don't waste the dead, he says sympathetically,
Come sit in my mouth.

Another poem, "Transformations," opens with the line, "In this house, death is a closet," and concludes, "I feel silent & changed, like a house / when the father dies." Elsewhere he sees "dead fathers circling the universe."

This death, he realizes, is not only for others: it is for himself. He is locked in the house of the dead with no key to salvation except his sex, his cunning, and his art. Metaphors of enclosure appear on almost every page—closets, rooms, caves, shells, the tube of the body. Another syndrome projects images of suffocation and drowning. In one climactic moment ("What Keeps You Thinking") the self burrows through the self: "A deep winding hole. / As you squeeze through yourself all night / you feel the pressure letting go."

Ryan's commitment is to seek exact verbal equivalents for ambiguous inner states. In reading certain of his lines one can almost detect the *frisson* of the poet when he hits it right:

Even thought was clear, like watching a lover
explore the bottom of a deep lake.

*

I'm honestly grateful there's breath
to make noise with, and many words
have meaning. I feel lucky
when hello doesn't hurt.
On a bus, I could love anyone.

*

I say she does belong. I say sometimes
I'm not alone, even if love imposes
its limits like a gangleader and this razor
of a brain makes me the enforcer.

*

You think constantly
of silk, how it must feel good
as the skin melts, lying there,
eyes rolled inward, looking at yourself.

*

Imagining pain, you wear out your body
slowly, like a favored article.

*

Still, those wings inside you.
At the hot stove all day you feel yourself
rising, the kids wrapping themselves
around your legs oh it's sexual
this nourishing food for the family
your father stumbling through the door
calling to you Honey I'm home.

The poems have their separate identities, but at
the same time they exist in an elaborate system of
cross-references. This room of any poem is like
that room, "a closet of secrets"; at every window
the moist animals of the night are nuzzling; the
same blind swimmer propels himself underwater
from page to page; nobody can stop the dead
father from walking. Few young poets have con-
structed so self-contained a world.

The sound of the verse is mostly desperate, but
it is not a leaden or a sodden desperation. A subtle
and mercurial persona inhabits this poetry of
interiors, subject to periodic crises of the spirit,
responsive to every metabolic change of weather.
In the passage that gives the book its title Ryan
writes:

We're learning how to walk unlit streets,
to see threats instead of trees,
the right answer to a teenager
opening his knife. The answer is yes.
Always we couldn't do otherwise.

("Prothalamion")

The landscape here is characteristically emblematic, but the danger is real. What matters is survival.

Most contemporary poets are attached to particulars; their act of the imagination depends on a concatenation of perceptions; they draw their sustenance from the visible universe. Ryan, on the contrary, is enamored of ideas, as well as of more conventional objects of desire, and rejoices in the capacity of the intellect to reason, to make fine discriminations, to move toward some tentative order, to categorize, to achieve the hard-edged beauty of abstraction. He is a poet who can speak of "kissing a concept," who is tempted by "the violence of strict edges," who acknowledges that "the other desire" (after sex) is "to sharpen the brain / to a fine edge." In "A Posthumous Poetics," which reviews, not without a touch of self-mockery, the history of his aesthetics, he speaks of "abstractions insisting on their fine edges, / asking to be used to open cans," and appropriately concludes with an example: "our first kiss, perfect as gravity."

Ryan does not usually conceive his poems in dramatic terms. When he does, as in "Lincoln Inward" and "The Janitor's Coffin," the protagonists emerge as aspects of the poet's own identity. The rhetorician who wonders how he sounds exposes his vulnerability: "I begin to listen to myself freeing the slaves: don't come back, I say, don't come back." The janitor who, like Pluto, is lord of the dead and the lower world, carries shapes of words in his nocturnal rounds that connect like a ring of keys. Essentially the structure of the poems is dialectical, as of a man conducting a running argument, or at least an urgent dialogue, with himself. Ryan's deceptively colloquial inflections oppose an abstract vocabulary, without excluding it, and resist, without negating, the formal pattern. In his usual strategy he tries to set the measure and tone of a poem, its integrity, with the very first line, to be tested against the flow and momentum of the syntax. He is adept at preserving the tension of the line and at controlling the tone.

In "Negatives," his most ambitious poem, he explores the meaning of a relationship with a woman in a sequence of thirty octaves that suggests a sonnet cycle. What he discovers in the process of composition, as he lets his poem think about itself, is the degree of denial in him. Hence the title, which may also be construed in its photographic sense. Throughout "Negatives" the focus is on the loved one, but another presence insists on getting into the picture:

> Let me say a word for orgasm
> which isn't death, but don't we speak
> as relief from the loneliness of sex,
> me feeling like a crowd as I push
> toward a way out of my body,
> you saying my name as if my name
> could let you in. I'm the stranger
> who rubs against you & grins.
> . . . .
> Let me put this straight:
> if I taste my death in the back
> of my mouth, don't expect a kiss.

It comes out in every word,
crawling through breath like a whip.
I believe it more than my life,
because more desperate, this friend,
my big woman, the only fact.

Threats Instead of Trees is an obsessive book,
producing in at least one reader intermittent
sensations of vertigo and claustrophobia, but it is
redeemed from narrowness and made strangely
exhilarating by the mobility of Ryan's mind. "As
soon as the mind is involved," Valéry once
observed, "everything is involved." He under-
stood, as his own work demonstrated, the aesthetic
possibilities of monomania: "I can see for my part
that the selfsame subject, and even the selfsame
words, could be taken up again and again,
indefinitely, and could occupy the whole of a
lifetime."

Not only does Michael Ryan let his poems
think about themselves; he gives them rope
enough, without letting go, to think about the
mind that is making them and its load of memo-
ries. He may be on the way to fulfilling a
prophetic sentence from one of Wallace Stevens's
letters: "The pleasures of poetry are not yet the
pleasures of thought; perhaps that is the work
poetry must do in the future."

STANLEY KUNITZ

I

The Myth

For a long time, nothing happened.
Then ancestors whispering, then fragments
of a forgotten life disturbing ordinary actions:
handling a stone, or bathing
you might think of the brain as a diamond.
Even thought was clear, like watching a lover
explore the bottom of a deep lake.
Everyone became friends,
imitating each other's most personal gestures.
The leaders said this happiness
is round like bowls, and devised simple rituals
in which touch wasn't a form of searching—
breasts, especially, seemed to return everything.

Still, some looked for damage
in the hard scars on our bodies.
They reminded us of the years of boredom,
when no sex meant no expectations,
and each object that hurt us
was a way to penetrate the skin.
Shouldn't we be ashamed?
Isn't this history we imagine:
in that one's ugly movement
of his arms? Her clumsy legs?

Although resisting privacy,
we began to see less distinctly.
Sometimes, during an intimate talk,
you'd swear you caught your best friend
closing his eyes, as in disappointment
with his own reflection.

So we tried exhaustion, swimming alone
for days. Slowly we noticed our bodies
becoming smooth & beautiful,
and the air seemed less necessary
the further you dove. Maybe
you'd forget you were actually underwater,
discovering, as you did, an old lover
reluctantly letting you go.

Transformations

1

In this house, death is a closet.
Already a stranger who isn't my father
has gone downstairs to open it:
he returns gradually, in a stale, heavy coat.
Does he unzip his face like a skirt?
He touches me so exactly, it might be a thought.

2

Now I'm older. My old mother
asks me to watch her skin fall off.
She knows I enter my wife slowly
to inhabit myself, like darkness
filling a closet as the door closes.
Accept your secrets, she says.
I worship her, I kiss her terrible wounds.

3

For a thirst, she offers the caress;
for itches, threats. I'm no idiot,
this means I'm a husband, bargaining
with my private needs for someone to go to.
It never works, although the child arrives.
Downstairs, that last musty touch . . .
I feel silent & changed, like a house
when the father dies.

Prothalamion

The love we define for ourselves
in terms of privacy, in suffering,
keeps each of us lonely as a fist,
but sometimes I might be arguing
with myself, you're that correct:
the hand inside me squeezes the word
intimacy until meaning a happy ending.
Perhaps this was also defined,
but driving at night, the shadows
on a drawn curtain meant terrible lives:
a father stuck in a job, his daughter
opening her blouse to strangers.

I'm afraid of marriage.
Your hands, for example, like a warm liquid
on my face don't evaporate
as you take them away.
Nor are those accidents silent,
the cut ones, or bodies crushed by trucks,
although we listen only in passing.
We're learning how to walk unlit streets,
to see threats instead of trees,
the right answer to a teenager
opening his knife. The answer is yes.
Always we couldn't do otherwise.

Speaking

I'm speaking again
as the invalid in a dark room.
I want to say thank you
out loud to no one.
I want to fold my hard arms in
on the sound, as the sound
dissolves slowly like a man living.

I'm honestly grateful there's breath
to make noise with, and many words
have meaning. I feel lucky
when hello doesn't hurt.
On a bus, I could love anyone.

It's not terrible to be alone.
Last night I talked to a person
so carefully I might have been looking
for a word that wouldn't change.
That made her ready for anything.

Really, I'm not being funny.
There are people everywhere sorry
for the pleasure that keeps them going,
although they circle that pleasure
like a herd around its dying leader.
This pleasure, for me, is in speaking,
as if words enclosed the secret
in myself that lasts after death.

The Poetry of Experience

for Skoyles & Bodnar

This poem comes from complete sorrow
and asks almost nothing of itself.

The situation is this: a woman I love
has been gone for three weeks.
At first there was an elation,
no more bad fights, then boredom
and the stricter need for affection.

Tonight I got drunk with a good friend.
We talked for hours about the sadness
of sad things, the sadness of women
because we must use them.
When the bar closed, we visited
two dumb girls. Sex was out of the question.

Now I'm alone with the radio on:
the story of a man who tried suicide
with soft lead bullets, shooting his head
four times before realizing
he could aim at the heart.

If I write this only for myself,
it is also to touch my life.
And you, whose life is worse,
to feel genuinely sorry for yourself.

Pastoral

The trees bending in wind like inflections
in our discussion of love, that widow

lifting her underclothes to show how lonely
she has been, and you do speak to her

if only to say yes we're very different
my husband is so gentle these evenings,

as through the window above our headboard
the animals wash each other for sleep,

the dead ones entering that easy movement
or our discussion of love only as inflections

like trees bending in the wind.

A History of Rooms

If chairs speak,
they don't tease us with stories
of a man tired of himself,
or the couple who formed possible
arrangements out of boredom.

Even the overstuffed one,
resting in the corner like an old god,
might tell us nothing.
So we make a history of rooms
to enclose our memory of each other,
as if through hours of description
we could imagine who we are.

In the last room, we were lovers.
I say, the mattress was on the floor,
if that means anything.
You insist there were noisy springs.
We agree it doesn't matter.

Where did we go wrong?
By the bureau, fixing your hair,
you catching my reflection in the mirror
as I look away once and for all?

This, then, as a scar on any furniture,
or the exclusion of a locked door.

The Latent Image

1

He does not go out.
He loves the consolation
of an imagined person, mistaking identity
for affection. What's missing is a woman
who has learned to accept slight gestures.
She does not demand.
Silently & without embarrassment, she does not demand.

2

You're kissing a concept.
The indistinct sound which surrounds it
comes from your throat. Even words appear
as one rich smell on the fingertips.
You stick them in your mouth.
Nothing happens, losing somebody,
bedding down without.

3

Say each person is a latent image
of the lives of the past.
Say a cool knowledge arrives
with death, as water over fever,
what happens to love?
Keep talking,
the dead wait for your answer.

4

I won't call you an angel or animal.
Your silence is violent,
the thing not to be named.
I can't deal with it, I corner you
to watch for teeth, turn my back
hoping you'll float away singing,
sleep, without ever having done enough.

5

All night she's disappearing,
gradual as dawn. He has imagined her
as darkness, afraid to lose obsessions
or to sleep without thought.
Faintly, she tosses a kiss
like a real lover as the day comes on.
Now something else takes over.

Room

Desire itself is movement
Not in itself desirable.

Burnt Norton

1

The violence of strict edges, a man
between his needs, and in this corner
he's uncomfortable, as if wanting
a stranger. Isn't it possible
he might contain these urges?
And what about the last borders?
Who will match touch for touch?
These are questions the room asks.

2

Not insects on the lips,
not animals staring at their tracks,
nothing human, no accessible location:
there is, however, the solid door
which suggests a reluctant exit
of desire, and perhaps keys fitting locks
whisper Resist. When you hear this,
you listen to someone else in pain.

3

Room supposes space: the guests
arriving, the usual nervous flirtation
until a woman walks in who accepts
the hard posture in corners.
Then the atmosphere is final,
no one recalls what isn't here,
no one notices the man behind her
who stands absolutely still.

Two Looks at Time

I. A Clock

One moment the woman appears
who invites what can be said,
such as my thin elusive description
of the funny twinge of satisfaction
when my best friend cried to me
over his wife leaving, and me happy
to accept my ability to be ugly.

This woman, I think, despises love
while taking my love in, "love"
as concept specifically felt by her
as a clock might feel the iota of dust
which ruins it, and she is that clock
because "woman" includes any time passing,
the time of sleep, perhaps, when brain
takes over body and I desire nothing.

So I wouldn't tell her about time,
but she appeared for one moment
as my body in a dream, displaying
in herself the slow breakdown of the heart
in one moment, as if to say this death
never ends, keep talking, you're speaking
to your complete inclusion.

But outside of dreams I'm tied
to situation, and return to my friend
crying in my arms, his wife upstairs
packing, and my desire for our division.
The woman welcomes those helpless words
I tell him. She won't love anything
that counts which will not be ruined.

2. *Belonging*

The other desire: to sharpen the brain
to a fine edge I'd turn on myself.
The figure, of course, doesn't suffice
and neither am I now that desperate:
I am aware of good times waking up,
sunlight filling the room like affection,
and perhaps an absolutely tangible woman
lies over my chest as if belonging.

I say she does belong. I say sometimes
I'm not alone, even if love imposes
its limits like a gangleader and this razor
of a brain makes me the enforcer.
Still, talking to her in this early hour,
I might enter the only possible metaphor
that moves us into the other's body forever.
The first desire is to become her lover.

What Keeps You Thinking

Caves.
The deep paths through a shell.
Remembering the fact of your death
you try to black in those holes,
as if every absence were terrible:
the long push of history
is inside you, although you don't see its shadow.
Could you fly out of yourself
as a screech? Or fade painfully
like an obsolete animal.

For awhile you might think of oceans,
imagining clarity, the waves flattening constantly
in one place touch means something,
but even whole objects, say both sides of ships,
sail away relaxed as a smooth so what.
You always pretend you're a place:
your house as a child
where the cellar was a mouth,
the desert you've never been to,
a beach, the sun tongueing your skin
like a woman, because without a landscape
isn't thought inhuman?
You want to make up a mountain
high enough to wipe out the margin
between the solid sky & sea,
but finally you'd miss that edge.

Tonight it's caves.
You wouldn't be something small
or absent, but a pure instrument:
a muscle. A deep winding hole.
As you squeeze through yourself all night
you feel the pressure letting go.
You feel the cells come apart
as you arrive a slow liquid,
those animals that live in real darkness
gather & give off the signal.

The Beginning of Sympathy

So close I'm defenseless,
I inhale my father's last breath:
it sticks, did I steal it,
this secret to begin myself.
Here is the secret at work:
a life fixed in its abstract immensity
that demands the usual journey:
the trees leaning close
whispering Don't worry we'll tell you something,
a big sun dropping announcements
of the unimaginable loneliness of guilt.
That is, in an otherwise normal landscape,
when you'd crawl away from your father
and have no thoughts, say to a hill
where the air's so pure it's visible,
objects become arbitrary & statements false.

Until the woman shows up
to show you origin, in a touch which shocks
like entering another person's dream,
but worth the connection to examine
the chink in yourself you stepped out of
to get here, rubbing her gently as a weapon,
this oh-so-welcome terminal salvation
I'd now compare to awakening.

Since she desires nothing, then, she's a phantom,
but finally I don't feel bad
because this ending approaches a beginning:
I've never left my father.
He's getting colder,
his voice thin as an angel's,
although his tongue is stuck in death.
Don't waste the dead, he says sympathetically,
Come sit in my mouth.

A Posthumous Poetics

From embarrassment, I made statements.
Those objects, tight caves & mouths, stuck together
briefly like dry lips, like a lover's insults.
The fact is they were ugly to all of us.
I said, How painstakingly personal!
Here are the words for this,
relentless as insects! I was hysterical.

Every tone became formal,
the worst urges nuzzling like housepets
for someone to feel them, each real subject
demanding more relaxed context for remarks.
Then abstractions insisting on their fine edges,
asking to be used to open cans,
or alone in the bathroom at bedtime.
Even then, I knew you'd leave them,
because who can stand such comparisons?

I learned to love this isolation
as a woman who appears to listen.
All night I'd talk about my life
anticipating her dramatic relief,
believing the affectionate gestures fill in
what isn't spoken. At those times
she seemed so genuine & friendly,
a voice inside the body
describing my hesitant surrender
as our first kiss, perfect as gravity.

II

Talking About Things

for Jon Anderson

For a moment, the idiot inside me who shouts *death* constantly blacks out & here I am, hobnobbing with objects: I ask myself, have you thanked the pillow for muffling that bickering? And what would I do without this fork to my hot pot pies? Good light bulbs, I appreciate not descending stairs in the dark . . .

Surely we all are included by objects, even if my shirt could care more about which body slides around inside it. From now on, let's only use nouns: knife, widow, fume, penis, idiot. Of course the little fellow's still unconscious. Yes I'll still call him *Man with a past which is not his* . . .

Lincoln Inward

I

I think I'm lying. Surely *one nation divided* implies another sad device of history, when I might have said *road into ourselves* and seemed friendly. This country nags me like a bad excuse, these critical days away from myself demanding accounts, looking at the future in my wife's sharp face.

II

Rutledge, if I lack faith, it's only an allegiance to the variety of breasts. Yes, there are injuries in sex. You can't sit with me in the box because of my egregious honesty, or the privacy which I speak. Still, when I enter you, I think *what's behind all this?*

III

One night I sleep with thought like a wife: the dreams become exciting, because who's thinking here, moving gently into my chest? She begins to take things apart: vocabulary, erections, the conditions of respect. I begin to listen to myself freeing the slaves: don't come back, I say, don't come back.

Cinderella as the Letter *C*

What are they looking for, that sadistic posse I call my family—while I, friendly, abscond in the basement eating old photographs of myself. Here's me at the moment of puberty in a zany fedora, another where I'm disguised as my father in his hidden encounter with a drudge. I don't know which is tastier . . . Meanwhile, Madge, the eldest sister, gallops to the cupboard for a cleaver, and Stepmother, that dross of slag, distributes climactic tools of torture. Have they discovered the ground glass with my name on it in their dinner? (The name means "boiling ashes" in German, everywhere I hear witches & slippers.) This is a rare pantoscopic of the whole clan up to their necks in mouse shit. I'm the one sucking a pumpkin, a little princess, a mere toddler, the last squirt of an enema, a vague placebo . . . That's it! Principium & lex! Here comes Stepmother to propound another enema! The family, those conceptual marauders, insists it will clear my head of these fantasies, chanting Fuck Cicisbeos and So may the relations of men be clipped—I'm royalty, you assholes! The polytechnic irreplaceable! I'm the plumcake on the cornmeal bottom!! Pants down, I'm a common woman squatting for violation, the years of hard usage tucked where even my prince would never come, oh ho, all my possible children fading to one clean odor of pleasure.

The Wrath of the Nincompoops

for Peter Michelson

First we take over the garbage, infiltrating empty cans of *Vesprey* & old maduros, crawling through foul pork, our feculent breath suggesting urges to the whole family. Mother, for example, begins to tingle wantonly while mopping, Junior whacks off behind his catcher's mitt each time he passes the kitchen . . . Then we slip into the open. Disguised as bagboys, we replace the price tags with obscene flags which parody the consumer's useless history. People wanting cereal get a boxful of lips, smokers split instantly into packs of miniature dildos, insomniacs believe we wandered through their last good dream . . .

In a top-secret report, the FBI insists we're meeting in someone's uterus. A team of crack surgeons performs mass hysterectomies, but no luck. The president becomes delirious, although maintaining that strict, ineffable silence. Meanwhile, the frozen pizzas dance & sing pornographic jingles when cooked. As a last-ditch maneuver, a liberal professor offers to eat the TV's & coshers himself to death. Another blockhead is elected on the promise to quash this nonsense, but by now no one cares. Nincompoopery sells! So we get fat jobs in advertising & become millionaires, those amputees trying to stop an oncoming train with a gesture . . .

Your Own Image

When by mistake you miss
the urinal in a public place,
there's no bending down, cleaning
up, or betting others won't
step in it. So you zip
your zipper with a flourish,
hoping the guy in the nearest
stall is admiring your follow
through & not the spreading puddle
which at least is your very own.
You stroll casually to the wash-
stand, avoiding thoughts
of barefoot little kids & cripples
whose leather laces brush
the floor and the curious eyes
that compare you to Pontius Pilate
as you wash your hands,
but you can't help meeting
your own image as you finish
the ablutions. It says,
You are dark and handsome.

Poem for Men Only

Astride pinnacles, the women aren't complaining
to the moon. Look, they're junking the cotton:
famous brand-name sanitary napkins snowball
down the mountain, blocking the major arteries
of our cities. The military suggests periodic
bombing; the president won't say anything.

But we see, don't we, we men shaking hands
in taverns: we've come home for years to empty houses,
the shock of no kiss, no dinner, a blank TV,
her dresses hanging in the closet like cloth suicides.
Every night we slide into bed alone, we're afraid
the pain we'll never know, we will never know.

Hitting Fungoes

Hitting fungoes to a bunch
of kids who asked me
nicely, I'm afraid the hard
ball they gave me might
shatter the stained-glass
window of the church
across this abandoned lot.
I see it all now, in
the moment the ball leaves
my hand before it smacks
the bat: we scatter
in every possible direction
but the pastor, sensing
a pervert, screams
to the cops to chase
the big one, and there
I am: trapped. I pull
my old Woodrow Wilson
Fellowship Letter out
of my worn suit pocket,
swing it wildly, but they
smell last night's sex
on my breath, condemn
me to jail for failure
to forget old needs or failure
itself. I swing without
thinking, the only way,
and the crack is the scream
of a hip-bone ripped

from its socket
on the rack. Not bad.
Not too deep, but a nice
arching loft. One kid,
who runs faster than the others,
makes a spectacular
diving catch & throws it back.

III

Letter from an Institution: I

The ward beds float like ghost ships
in the darkness, the night light
above my bed I pretend is a lighthouse
with a little man inside who wears
a sailor cap & tells good old stories
of the sea. The little man is me.
Perhaps I have a dog called Old Salt
who laps my hand & runs endlessly
down the circular stairs.
Perhaps we live in sin.
I dream of ships smashing the reefs,
their bottoms gutting out,
the crews' disembodied voices screaming
"Help us help us help somebody please"
and there is no one there at all
not even me. I wake up nervous,
Old Salt eating my flesh. I wake up nervous,
the canvas bedstraps biting my groin.
The night nurse, making the rounds,
says I bellow in sleep like a foghorn.

Letter from an Institution: II

Nothing moves at night
except small animals
kept caged downstairs
for experiments, going
bullshit, and the black
janitor's broom whisking
closer by inches.
In the ward, we all
have room for errors & elbows
to flail at excitement.
We're right above the morgue;
the ice boxes make our floor
cold. The animals seem to know
when someone, bored with holding
on, gives out: they beat
their heads & teeth
against the chicken wire
doors, scream and claw.
The janitor also knows:
he props his heavy broom
against his belt, makes
a sign over himself
learned from a Cajun,
leaves us shaking
in our bedstraps
to drag the still
warm & nervous body
down from Isolation.

Letter from an Institution: III

I have a garden here, shaped
like Marienbad, remember?,
I lose myself
in, it seems. They only look for me
sometimes. I don't like my dreams.

The nurses quarrel over where I am
hiding. I hear from inside
a bush. One is crisp
& cuts; one pinches. I'd like to push
them each somewhere.

They both think it's funny
here. The laughter sounds like diesels.
I won't move because I'm lazy.
You start to like the needles.
You start to want to crazy.

House

You don't sleep in the house
that stands for happiness. You dance

to the music of its cracks, flexing
your lonely muscles like a priest,

pretending your body is a ghost
come to haunt yourself. The closets,

with luck, remember you as moths
or shelves & kiss your open mouth

with years that taste like dust,
the attic's black as the cellar,

and the rooms, you discover, are all
the same room. You don't care.

You pick one & live there, dividing
the light & dark among the walls

you know will never scream, dying
to believe you are yourself

the origin of your dreams.

Little Political Poem

Our fathers choked themselves on speech.
You hear their dead howl in your cells

but luckily you set the alarm in time
for this dream & this dream changes:

the children fill your body like blood,
shouting "Let us be born tonight!"

It's morning. You wake up ready to fight.
The wife, in some lonely hour of sleep,

has turned away from you & you think
the light of another day makes her taut

& alive. Her breathing sounds like thought
until you realize you're still dreaming

that the war is really here, in the words
you know by heart, in the tight gap of your lips,

but you can't believe you hear the dead
howl of the children eating their way out

of the fathers, or the impossible string
of vowels caught in your throat like diamonds.

If you did, good citizen, could you listen?

Drowning

From this distance, the shore
shows up as a heart attack
and each thin line of reef means
brief connection & solidity.
Are you ever alone at sea?
What is close enough to touch?
The stroke you have called a kiss
flails in a breakneck pace
that includes no one, a rhythm
of panic you can't keep up
for brothers or wives or the history
which flows between your lips.

You remember learning to swim
by taste: the father you knew
would drown you, you tried
to climb with your teeth.
Unpried & held up for one quick
breath, the flesh exploded
in your mouth. When his blood
became the lines of your throat,
you were taught to live inside
a shout & to trust that life
as fact.

        Off the impossible
coast of Lagos, you recall
the calmness of the dead man's
float, but even that is work.

The jerking in your chest
is not a shape you recognize
or want. If only you could stand
by yourself! You imagine a darkness
at the bottom of some ocean
that is really black.

Flight

for Jack Myers

If the thought of the body is a map,
did I want to fly, white nerves & pure
shock, to the one full cell in my brain?
This plane I'm strapped in like the night
splits the tough sky & spreads its dark
legs, roiling black dust in the wake
like blood in the sea: each lonely wave
a dead limit someone talks at every day,
as if rage fused silence & distance.

In the last-ditch reach of memory,
I hear the noise of takeoff, not me.
I see buildings change to a pattern
of themselves, then to a pattern of farms
that must be real farms, if we'd dive in
close enough. I'd bail out to taste
the earth fill my mouth. I'd listen
to my voice & believe speech makes touch
inaccurate. I'd know dirt talks back.

My fat nerves say no. A kid sister
pokes her brother's head between her knees,
the stewardess dreams of bursting
her lacquered skin & outside the air
could freeze a man. Even the dull hum
of pressure does not squeeze out
the vague word that makes death possible.
Did I want to steam to the heart
like some dumb machine on tracks?
I'm going somewhere. Nothing distracts.

IV

The Meeting

for my father

Nothing is evidence. This shadow
you call your life cools the senses
like absence & you move toward it
instinctively because you think you feel
heat. You do. We meet. I talk
of hands, how they ask to be filled,
don't they, how they're first to be
touched, how we close into fists
in this darkness & speech is difficult.
I could be anybody but I'm not.

Aren't we objects in the light
of facts? If I say "cold" or "touch"
or "sun," don't you hear an alarm?
One real word explodes the earth
we've forgotten, the children were
always children, the space we know
hurts. Listen to our heavy bodies
blowing up: my tongue's a rocket.
Your eyes orbit the cold sun
like dead fathers circling the universe.

The Janitor's Coffin

A cold furnace. A closet of secrets.
A place to put away the body
like a shirt you don't wear again.
Still, death makes you careful.
You fuse speech like hot metal,
as if to cast a box of iron
around yourself, as if each sentence
were your last. The wife says
you're getting harder, you don't try
to talk. You say it hurts.
Your mouth closes like a cut.
You imagine shapes of words
in your brain when the heart
deflates & you go mute, whether
they connect like the ring of keys
strapped to your belt or if they open
locks.
        Sometimes, on night rounds,
you surprise two people behind a desk
breathing in each other's mouths.
You close the door, afraid.
The wife says you must be getting old,
letting something bother you.
It's true. You think constantly
of silk, how it must feel good
as the skin melts, lying there,
eyes rolled inward, looking at yourself.

The Blind Swimmer

for Thomas Lux

We know he's out there,
swimming slowly, searching for corners
in the sea where the dark has rubbed away.
He holds each breath like a last chance
at sleep, afraid of entering some insane
dream where voices without shapes scream
"Swim" and even the ocean is missing.
Still, he swims. The water fills his cupped hands
like breasts, a slight touch in a crowd
of waves pushing him nowhere, the blue
salt glued to his eyes like braille.
What do his dead eyes say?
The body that keeps him floating is a room,
the sun will stop if he just walks out?

On the shore, our feet planted like roots,
we watch for a sign. Some of us yell
at anything: a fat dolphin breaking the surface
for air; the edge of a seagull's wing
mistaken for a hand. The ocean doesn't stand for
our lives, calm & regular, but we still fear
drowning. So, safely together,
we wait for the blind swimmer
to walk out of the sea & say it's all right,
you can swim alone without seeing.
Some of us wait a long time.

I know he's out there.
He smells the ocean, doesn't he, that old
naked woman? She takes his tongue
in her mouth, doesn't her mouth open?
I hear him going under,
quietly as memory enters sleep, his memories
nothing I can imagine, tasting water so deep
light is terrible & fish see through their skin.

Sexual Energy

Someone else inside you.
A knot.
An old man tightening up.
In the rooms of his slim house
all night he talks to his shadow.
You think you hear the echo.
You think the stories of an old man's life
are real, although you make up the detail:
children he can't remember, for example,
or the woman he spilled like water.
Imagining pain, you wear out your body
slowly, like a favored article.

Doesn't he own the voice
cornering you into sleep
which doesn't fit in your mouth?
Always you roll toward the wife,
your wet tongue fluttering her lips
but still her old hard self.
Alone, the space between words is a gap
you could fall through forever,
but don't you love panic?
You try to be direct:
hatred of water
you admit, water won't be tied up,
you say. Water can relax.
You'd crack your chest like an egg,
the stiff insides, that pure idiot mystery,
dropped out open where you can see,
although wounded you still aren't a woman
and giving in means losing your skin.

But you give in.
Throwing back the covers,
you hover over your wife, hissing
you'll split her up the middle.
This is no old man talking.
Quietly, you feel yourself unravel.

Barren Poem

for Marvin Bell

All night the blind entrance of the children.
Where are they coming from, smelling of boiled milk,
their bodies sliding beneath each other
like fish? Because my wife hears noise,
I go down to the cellar to look.
Nothing moves. The air is damp with sex.
Animals no one has named
live here, the ones who become children,
who eat each other's eyes in our dreams.
I can't find them.
I would hook one by the mouth, its nerves
crawling up my hand like hot worms,
and rake its brain until it talked roots.
Does their absence follow me,
hidden as breath in speech?

Once upstairs, I talk:
in my old room
there's a bed where I curl up
& one light that burns holes in closed eyes.
Each time I call my mother
I get smaller & she will not help.
My wife has heard it before.
She won't ask for a child
alive inside her
although she holds my mouth to her breast.
She prefers me beneath her.
Breathless, I pretend to enter her with knives.

The Children's Room

She sneaks in here at night
because the walls don't talk & the children,
she says, are friends. I'm not.
She doesn't like me coming in, afraid
of saying what's what, saying
this darkness is an ocean
or the death we'll never touch. That is,
we're closed up. But it's more complex.

For instance, tonight I'm looking down her throat
the shadow of the ocean
like an immense animal shifting in sleep.
Herself inside herself, wanting to come out?
I can't explain that.

Maybe she's the ocean & I'm swimming,
this silence is a long intake of breath
I'm holding like a final kiss.
Wasn't the first man quiet?
Thinking of death, could he name it?

Fathers name things,
they can't help it. The children,
too young to speak, sweat out my words
in their sleep as if words were liquid & burn
down to salt. My children are filled with ocean,
I can't wait to hear how they tell it,
each new sound rolling from their mouths
as memories we finally connect.

Let's start over.
Wife, I'll call you water.
Your body contains waves
swallowing their shadows as they break
constantly, the waves a word
for our sane life that keeps coming back.
I admit I know nothing about light.

I want you to wake up.
Let's say I can hold you
like a solid in my own bed.
Let's say speech fits & makes sense.
And when you need an ending,
I'll read an old poem called "Drowning."

Flood

for my sister

Each house separate,
our lives priced in dry rooms
that don't tell secrets—
do you forget the space
we made of the family house,
brought up to read money & believe specifically?
Father drank in the basement, our family secret,
because "it's cool & damp."
But we never thought of water
inside us, or water anywhere—

Rita, I wanted his death.
I was afraid.
I wanted sleep
without those moist animals
beating against the windows with their teeth.
And now the first hard knock on your house
does wake you up
although you know it's real water
you can't stop. But you are moving,

gathering your own children instinctively
your hands wavering above them
like fish they're still breathing
you see them caught underwater
clinging to rocks with their mouths
you won't let it happen you'd swim
miles with them hanging on your neck . . .

Long-distance, I hear the flood's over.
You don't mention father:
your family safe, warped walls, the contaminated house . . .
You won't describe that fear
driving the last bridge & looking over the edge.
You say you were surprised
by the beauty of drowned pigs.

This Is a Poem for the Dead

fathers: naked, you stand for their big faces,
mouths stuffed flat, eyes weighted, your miserable dick
sticking out like a nose. Dressed, you're more
of a mother making dinner: those old dirt bags,
the lungs, sway inside your chest like tits
in a housedress. Perhaps you're frying liver
which shrinks like your father getting older.
You still smell him breathing all over
your skin. He drank himself to death.

Now each woman you meet is a giant.
You'd crawl up their legs & never come down.
Even when you think you're big enough
to touch them, his voice flies from under
your throat & "I love you" comes out
a drunk whimper. All you can do
is breathe louder. You're speaking
to the back of your mouth. Finally,
you admit you know nothing
about sex & drown the urge slowly
like a fat bird in oil.

Still, those wings inside you.
At the hot stove all day you feel yourself
rising, the kids wrapping themselves
around your legs oh it's sexual
this nourishing food for the family
your father stumbling through the door
calling to you Honey I'm home.

V

Negatives

for P

I should hug groups.
I want touch to represent
the quiet before my first heartbeat,
the sound of meetings to exude
from trees. Surround me, mothers,
I can't compete with the leaves
falling this autumn like results.
Tell the women in long coats.

———

Another day of objects.
If I love you, even the mirror
says it matters, much less the beds
suggesting a singular death.
Please don't mention the reprisals
inside our bodies as some operation
of nerves. Sure we're wearing down
and we don't see everything.

———

But even morning's dark
in closets, all my best shirts
arranged like familiar mistakes
that need someone to dress.
Crazy that I put the one on
which smells of you in heat,
the distraction of good nights,
coming at you, lights out.

I don't watch you dress.
I want something in my mouth.
Imitate a warm factory
at coffee break, machines turned off,
a snack wagon buzzing & the dirty jokes.
As I stroll in to inspect the work,
everything quiets: the scared one
inside you hands over his donut.

If continuity is an illusion
of motion, pretend we're running
home to an idea of ourselves
as a child in different clothes.
Perhaps mother removes your gloves
as she wraps me in hundreds of jumpsuits
so that now I sweat out this statement:
love, we don't go fast enough.

There are no close finishes.
The separations we measure
not by broken tape or watches
catch in our reticulate memory
which snaps because it has to.
So maybe I wipe out the past
now, when I can't speak to you,
with only so many words.

And no landscape makes sense.
The last time I visited the ocean
I expected to pay for it.
We watched the night coming back,
some gulls bed down on rocks,
a prison close by on an island
we could barely make out.
It was so close, I tried to be honest.

The switch to past tense as idea
or sensation become remnants,
I was here etched into a cliff,
for instance, stands for the loss
of occurrence when I couldn't love
someone else, good grasp on isolation
in scraping a rock for no reason,
because the words were fixed in myself.

Insane, this rubric of fuses:
I want to stamp our bad history
into each casual utterance
and mark this perpetual dullness.
I would say "apples are grenades"
but I'm afraid of connections,
and when you wake beside me each morning,
love, I feel like exploding.

This is no time for thought.
We're returning after work
too bored to talk, the slow drives
becoming dangerous, a traffic of idiots
in our mouths. Spit it all out.
Admit you'd do something vicious.
Tell me you really hate children
because they might be someone else.

———

Now the house away from water.
Now the germ carried in clothes.
What loving isn't disease,
our failures predictable as waves?
If I could make my body separate
from the memory of you naked,
each closet wouldn't breed infection.
Now let's talk about oceans.

———

When fish sprout wings they aren't birds,
and your sadness is a root.
At first we changed touches into facts,
nothing was private. Then tendrils
gathering like a nest:
evolution in the definite shape
of your hands covering your face,
when the only comfort is difference.

———

The country as tough guy.
Our problems. Take that big stick
and hit me until I don't know
pain from mistakes, or the words
for them. When you do me a favor,
love, make it slow as erosion
because we've given up plans.
Speaking politically, flowers are strange.

———

I admit it's silly to ask
who commands these murders.
Everywhere, bodies fall so gently
there must be no one to begin with,
as if this were the trick to dying.
Touch me like a corpse in autumn.
I admit it's becoming easier
to make someone disappear.

———

If my death is a negative,
I'm holding myself to a light
which burns it at the edges.
Still, the whites are black.
Still, a vague outline represents
me as a child floating back
like blood in a river, my mother
or father trying to take the picture.

———

So lines make pictures & why not?
Me in a hat in my father's shirt
comes out to my hanging on you
like a guilty kid, hiding the bad thing
I've done. When you aren't around
I feel myself relax,
doing nothing except talking
as if you were death.

———

This isn't the parable of the man
out of control on a snowmobile
although maybe I'm skidding merrily
through a forest until halted by myself
disguised as a bear in a scout hat
saying Only you can prevent suicides.
Today I admit I'm afraid of myself.
You say you don't believe in forests.

———

These dumb elations, a laughter
at nothing: I feel like an audience
the moment it enters a long silence,
as if the talk-show host inside me
were gradually breaking down.
For awhile I pretend it's another routine,
the jokes deliberate, covering
for the starlet who never shows up.

———

For you love's a question of range:
hunting it, at what distance
is it possible to be accurate.
You'd stretch out as that forest,
the trees breathing on your knife
like cats. No, rather a gunblast
that echoes across mountains, me
falling for miles like a big dumb bird.

———

Like the indifference at the center
of despair, you might be hidden
by the hard words for change
with which we hurt ourselves.
I want you to take it easy, say
"Fine, you're human" daily & care for me.
Then we'll look into these holes always
opening beneath us like a batch of throats.

———

When the animals watch our house
all night, shadows in fur moving
as I flip on more lights,
I console myself.
I think love is careful,
like touching a cage:
if I turned away from my window,
you wouldn't be here.

———

I want to be so alone now
that thought enters as a sound
of footsteps in an empty house
coming closer as I crouch here
holding my own hands thinking
that in fact I make you up
you're a way to approach myself
so now I want to be alone.

———

My translation of events
not into pain but characters
on a dim street, circling.
It isn't hard to guess the language
their cold knives speak,
as if describing an ugly thought.
Sometime they'll stop me, I think,
as I pass untouched & empty as light.

———

I'm tired of mystery & statements
and I'm sick of being a wiseass.
Back in the house where I grew up
I think I've never been myself.
In the closet, everything's arranged
in two's: 2 hardballs, 2 statues of Christ . . .
O double concussion! O pairs of breasts!
One person isn't enough.

———

These random objects from my past
aren't hooks, do you think,
because I love to watch myself
harden like a poisoned fish:
beached, drying out, and empty.
If memory also acts as poison,
to watch you return is a pleasure.
Don't say the pain comes later.

———

All this edged by seriousness
because you give me coherence
as if tired of gifts. We're nice
together, wearing each other like flowers,
and the moment of picking this fight
might hurt. So because it's Christmas,
you slam doors & yell Fuck off,
because being nice is boring.

———

Let me say a word for orgasm
which isn't death, but don't we speak
as relief from the loneliness of sex,
me feeling like a crowd as I push
toward a way out of my body,
you saying my name as if my name
could let you in. I'm the stranger
who rubs against you & grins.

———

The solutions pass like seconds,
they are that specific. First
my childhood shows up as a father
I want to love, adolescence
in the back seat, and friends
leaving. Maybe I hate women,
but even old ideas tick off.
The problem is to notice a loss.

———

Let me put this straight:
if I taste my death in the back
of my mouth, don't expect a kiss.
It comes out in every word,
crawling through breath like a whip.
I believe it more than my life,
because more desperate, this friend,
my big woman, the only fact.

———

Where are the openings in skin
a shadow can't fit through?
This light inside closed hands
isn't emotional, but I want an image
to stand for the places I go to
within my body, leaning toward death:
a female shape to wind through veins.
All night I have not said I love you.

C51335

PS3568
Y39T48   Ryan, Michael, 1946–
                Threats instead of trees.   Foreword by Stanley Kunitz.
         New Haven, Yale University Press, 1974.

                  xviii, 66 p.   21 cm.   (Yale series of younger poets, v. 69) $6.00

         I. Title. II. Series.

         PS3568.Y39T48   811'.5'4   73–87737
         ISBN 0-300-01738-3; 0-300-01739-1 (pbk.)

         Library of Congress   74 [4]